NADIYA'S

Bake Me a Story Celebration

NADIYA'S

Bake Me a Story Celebration

Nadiya Hussain

illustrated by Clair Rossiter

Hodder

HODDER CHILDREN'S BOOKS

First published in Great Britain in 2018 by Hodder and Stoughton

1 3 5 7 9 10 8 6 4 2

A CIP catalogue record for this book
is available from the British Library.

ISBN 978 1 444 93958 3

Edited by Emma Goldhawk
Art Directed by Alison Padley

Photography by Adam Lawrence
Food photography by Georgia Glynn Smith
Food styling by Lisa Harrison

Printed and bound in Europe
by Mohn Media Mohndruck GmbH

The paper and board used in this book
are made from wood from responsible sources

FSC
www.fsc.org

MIX
Paper from
responsible sources
FSC® C104740

Hodder Children's Books
An imprint of
Hachette Children's Group
Part of Hodder and Stoughton
Carmelite House
50 Victoria Embankment
London EC4Y 0DZ

An Hachette UK Company
www.hachette.co.uk

www.hachettechildrens.co.uk

To the person missing from this book – I miss your smile in the folds of these pages. But I have the honour of seeing that smile for real, everyday. To my boy. The biggest heart, biggest feet and the wisest owl I know. This one is for you, Musa.

Hi guys!

So good to see you here. Would you like to say 'hi' to the other two little people on the opposite page? They would like to say hi to you!

I'm Nadiya and these are my kids, Dawud and Maryam. You may remember us from my first two books, *Bake Me a Story* and *Bake Me a Festive Story*. There's one person missing this time, and that's my boy Musa. He grew up a little while I was writing this book, and although he's not here, he says hi too!

No matter how big my kids get, we love to cook together and share stories as a family. We love doing crafts too!

In *Bake Me a Celebration Story*, you will find brand-new recipes, stories and poems about special moments of celebration from around the world. We even have some fun crafts that will keep your hands and your mind busy.

You could try the recipe or craft first, and then read the story or poem, or you could enjoy reading while your bakes are in the oven or the paint is drying on your craft. It doesn't matter which way round you do it; all that matters is that you enjoy yourself.

I always love to see my readers' bakes and makes, so don't forget to use #BakeMeAStory when you post pictures on social media!

So, pop on your apron, get the glitter ready and join us for a whole year of celebrating!

Love, Nadiya xxxx

Maryam

Dawud

HELPFUL HINTS AND TASTY TIPS

Safety in the kitchen

Always make sure a grown-up is with you in the kitchen.

Don't touch the kitchen knives – they are sharp! If a grown-up says you can use them to chop or slice, be very careful.

Ask a grown-up to help you if you are using a food processor.

Always wash your hands in warm soapy water before you start.

Be careful of the hot oven and hobs.

Oven temperature

All the recipes in this book have been tested in a fan-assisted oven. If you are using a conventional oven, increase the temperature by 20°C.

Measurements

g – grams
ml – millilitres
tsp – teaspoon
tbsp – tablespoon
°C – degrees celsius

Recipe guide

Every recipe has a guide to show you how easy or difficult it might be.
Always make sure a grown-up is with you when you try any of these
recipes, especially when it needs a knife or a food processor, or involves
anything hot.

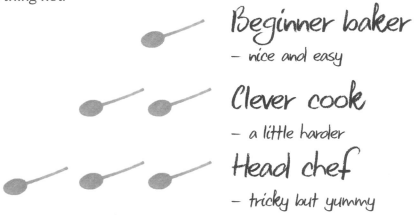

Beginner baker
– nice and easy

Clever cook
– a little harder

Head chef
– tricky but yummy

CONTENTS

Chinese New Year

NIAN NO MORE

There was once a very small village that sat between two mountains. It was so small and so remote and so hidden, you had to stand on one leg at the foot of the mountain with your hands in the air to get a mobile signal.

The village was a lovely place, with lovely people in it. But there were only two hundred villagers living there and every year the numbers dropped. Families would move in and then leave not long after.

There was one big problem with living in that village – on the first day of every year, without fail, a massive swarm of locusts would rip through the streets and destroy everything. They would eat all the veggies in the village vegetable patches and all the flowers in people's gardens – even the garden hedges would be devoured. The locals called them the Nian locusts, after a legendary, fearsome creature called the Nian. No one had ever

seen the Nian, but all children learned about it in the stories their grandparents told them.

The two hundred villagers (now one hundred and eighty after last year's invasion) decided they really needed to be prepared this year.

One day, Yuyan was helping her grandfather make some spring rolls. Yuyan's grandfather was the only person who had been living there since the village was built.

"Those locusts really are hungry, aren't they, grandfather?" she said.

"Yes, little one, they are," her grandfather replied, gloomily. "They might be hungry, but I really wish they wouldn't eat my prize-winning dahlias every year."

Yuyan was determined to help her grandfather and his beloved flowers, but she didn't know what to do. She wandered to the edge of the village and called out into the mountains in frustration.

"What do I do to get rid of the locusts? Somebody help me!"

As expected, there was no reply, and Yuyan went home feeling a bit sad.

Later that evening, the phone went. Yuyan's grandfather answered.

"This is Nian Pest Control," came a voice at the other end of the phone.

"Pardon? Did you say Nian?" Yuyan's grandfather was shocked. "Can you help us? We have a Nian problem and the new year is tomorrow."

Yuyan rushed over to listen in to the call.

"The Nian does not like the colour red," the voice said. "Nor dragons."

Yuyan couldn't believe it – she had just made a red dragon from loo rolls at school that day. It would be perfect for protecting her grandfather's dahlias from the Nian locusts.

Yuyan and her grandfather went to every house in the village to teach them how to make a loo-roll dragon, then they settled in for the evening with a fresh batch of spring rolls to eat and their dragon in their window. It was that night that the locusts would come.

They woke the next morning, scared to open the curtains. But when they did, they couldn't believe their eyes. For the first time, there were no missing vegetables and all the garden hedges in the village were intact. Best of all, Yuyan's grandfather's dahlias were definitely not chomped on.

They were ecstatic. Yuyan took her grandfather to the place between the mountains and they both called out a simple thank you. It was the happiest new year they had ever had.

From that day forward, every home in the village made a loo-roll dragon the night before new year, and the Nian locusts were never seen again.

SPRING ROLLS

These spring rolls are great because you can put them in your hand and eat them while you're on the move. They are an excellent way to get more veggies into your tummy, too!

Makes 14

Ingredients

3 tbsp olive oil, plus a little more for baking (optional)

400g skinless chicken thigh fillets, thinly sliced

½ tsp Chinese five spice

1 tbsp tomato ketchup

1 tbsp soy sauce

300g bag of sliced stir-fry vegetables

juice of ½ lime

large handful of coriander, roughly chopped

1 tbsp black sesame seeds

1 box of filo sheets (7 sheets)

1 egg, lightly beaten

oil spray (optional)

sweet chilli sauce (optional)

salt and pepper

Method

- Pop a large non-stick frying pan on the hob, add the oil and heat over a medium to high heat. When the oil is hot, add the chicken and cook for 5–6 minutes, until lightly golden.

- Add the five spice, ketchup and soy sauce. Cook the mixture for 5 minutes, making sure to stir.

- Now tumble in all the vegetables and mix.

- Add the lime juice, reduce the heat slightly and cook until there is no more liquid in the bottom of the pan, stirring frequently. This should take about 10 minutes over a medium to low heat.

- Once it is cooked, transfer the mixture to a large bowl and allow to cool.

- When it has cooled, add the coriander and sesame seeds and mix through. Check the seasoning and add salt and pepper to taste.

- Preheat the oven to 200°C fan/gas mark 7 and get a baking tray ready.

- Take the filo sheets and lay them out. Cut down the centre of the pile of pastry to make 14 square-ish sheets of filo.

- Take each square and set at an angle so a point is facing you. Add 1 heaped tablespoon of the mixture towards the lower end.

- Fold over the lower point to cover the filling.

- Now take the right corner of pastry and fold it over the filling, then take the left corner of the pastry and fold that over the filling, too.

- Gently roll the pastry upwards and a spring roll should start to form. Before you get to the end, brush the highest point of the square with the beaten egg and finish rolling to seal.

- Pop the spring roll onto the baking tray, then repeat to form all the spring rolls.

- Spray or brush with oil and bake for 15–20 minutes until golden brown. I like to serve these with sweet chilli sauce, but they are also delicious on their own. Just be careful not to eat them right away, because the filling will be scorching hot.

LOO-ROLL DRAGON

You will need:

1 loo-roll tube

red paint

paint brush

scissors

red, yellow and orange tissue paper

PVA glue

small and large red pompoms

googly eyes

To make:

Paint the loo roll red and leave it to dry completely.

Cut thin strips of tissue paper, each about 1.5cm wide. Glue the strips to the inside of one end of the dry loo roll.

At the same end, glue the small pompoms to the top of the loo roll to make the nostrils.

Now stick the googly eyes to the large pompoms and add to the other end of the loo roll for the eyes.

Leave to dry, then make the dragon breathe flames by blowing through the loo roll, or using a hairdryer on a very gentle setting! ROAAARRRR!

I read everywhere about Valentine's.

It's a day about love between a pair.

It's for showing just one special person.

Exactly how much that you care.

One day to show them your feelings.

One day to make them feel great.

One day they'll feel butterflies in tummies.

And not 'cause of something they ate!

But something about Valentine's bothers me.
And my confusion will not go away!
Why is the love that I have in my heart
Just for one person, one day?

That doesn't seem fair to me, mummy.
How is that caring? I cried
I know lots of very nice people.
And I'm bursting with love deep inside.

Will you be my Valentine, mummy?
Oh, hang on, I can't forget Daddy…
Or my friends up the road, or my sister!
And what about Granddad and Nani?

I've so many spare hugs and kisses,
'I love yous' for people to hear.
I can't share it all in one single day.
It would take me the whole of the year!

Valentine's Day celebrates love on February 14th and is named after Saint Valentine. In Ancient Rome, the emperor put Saint Valentine in prison when he tried to arrange marriages for lonely soldiers.

If Valentine's Day is for caring.
A time when you say 'I love you',
Why wait for the 14th of February?
Share Valentine's love all year through!

LOVE HEARTS PUPPY CHOW

This is the perfect treat to eat with someone you love, as you'll be sharing out of one bowl. Puppy chow is a snack popular in the United States – it is crispy cereal covered with melted chocolate. I've snuck in some Love Hearts too, in honour of Valentine's Day.

Makes 1 large bowl

Ingredients

100g cornflakes

200g white chocolate

1 tbsp unsalted butter

39g tube of Love Hearts

2 tbsp heart sprinkles, or sugar stars

1 tbsp icing sugar

Method

- Measure out the cornflakes into a large mixing bowl.

- Add the white chocolate to a separate large microwaveable bowl and microwave for 1 minute. Stir, then microwave in 10-second bursts, stirring each time, until the chocolate is liquid.

- Add the butter to the liquid chocolate and mix it in until melted.

- Pour the melted mixture over the cornflakes and stir until all the flakes are covered.

- Add the Love Hearts and the sprinkles and mix through. Some will stick to the flakes and others will be loose – that's okay.

- Leave to cool, then pop it all into a zip-lock freezer bag.

- Now add the icing sugar, seal the bag and toss it all around until fully dusted and powdery.

- Pour into a large bowl and dig in!

PASTRY ROSES

These will be the prettiest treats you will ever make. They are so pretty you might not want to eat them ... But, they are also pretty yummy, so you should manage it okay! Who would you like to give a pastry rose to?

Makes 12

Ingredients

4 tbsp lemon juice

3 small red apples

plain flour, for dusting

2 sheets of ready-rolled puff pastry, chilled

2 tbsp seedless raspberry jam

25g unsalted butter, melted

1 tbsp icing sugar, for dusting

You will also need:

cupcake cases, in green foil if possible

Method

- Half fill a large bowl with water then add the lemon juice. This mixture will stop the apples going brown.

- Now cut each apple in half, take out and throw away the core and slice the apple as thinly as you can. Drop the slices straight into the lemony water, making sure they are submerged and topping up with as much water as you need to cover them.

- Now microwave the bowl on a high heat for 5 minutes. This will cook the apples just enough to make them easy to twist and soft enough to bend.

- Take out and drain the apples. Set aside.

- Line a 12-hole muffin tray with cupcake cases. I like to use green foil ones so you can't see butter seeping through and they look like the underside of a rose.

- Dust a work surface with flour and roll out the pastry sheets a little more to make them slightly thinner. Cut each into six lengthways, to make 12 long strips in total.

- Mix a splash of water with the jam to make it a little runnier, then brush jam along each strip.

- Now take the apple slices and lay them, slightly overlapping, across the top half of the pastry strip, so the red skin is facing out.

- Now take the bottom half of the pastry strip and fold over the apple. Starting at one end, roll the strip inwards to make a beautiful rose.

- Pop into a cupcake case.

- Once you have made all 12 roses, put the muffin tray into the fridge for 30 minutes to chill the pastry. Preheat the oven to 180°C fan/gas mark 6.

- Remove the roses from the fridge and brush them all over with melted butter.

- Bake for 35-40 minutes. Leave to cool in the tin for at least 30 minutes.

- Sift over the icing sugar and serve.

Nadiya's tip:
If I'm giving these away as a present, I like to put them in a box, scrunch up some green tissue paper and arrange them like a posy of flowers.

It was a warm and sticky day. It was even warmer and stickier than you might imagine, as this story happens in a place called Lahore, which is in Pakistan. Now imagine being in Lahore on a warm and sticky day, sitting in the middle of a classroom. It was warm and sticky and distracting. Especially for two certain children, Zaid and Zoya.

Zaid and Zoya were twins, and they got up to mischief any chance they got. After lunch, it was time for History. Zaid and Zoya didn't like History. They loved Art, it was their favourite lesson of all time. But History … not so much.

"Miss, whyyyyy do we have to do History?" groaned Zaid.

"Miiiisssss, it's old and boring and nobody cares," Zoya said.

The twins' teacher, Miss Ahmed, put her hands on her hips and nodded at the banner on the other side of the room. Printed in gigantic letters was the message, 'History never looks like history when you are living through it'.

"What do you say? Shall we give history a chance?" Miss Ahmed said to Zaid and Zoya with a wink.

The twins looked at each other and shrugged.

Miss Ahmed began, "Children, I want you to close your eyes and imagine something for me. Think about the markets around us here in Lahore. Now think of them in the past, when for one day every year they were filled up with yellow. Yellow clothes, yellow scarves, yellow kites ... Now imagine the delicious scent of ladoos and cherry biscuits in the air ... Mmmm, yummy."

The classroom fell silent. Miss Ahmed had everyone's attention. Even the twins. Even though they didn't like History.

"Go on, Miss Ahmed, you were saying ..." said Zoya.

"I have just set the scene for a festival. The ancient Basant Kite Festival, or Jashn-e-Baharan," Miss Ahmed continued.

Zaid and Zoya's teacher told them wonderful stories about the Basant Kite Festival from days gone by, until, DRIIIIIINNNNNG! the bell rang.

"Okay, class, off you go," Miss Ahmed said. "We will find out more about this wonderful festival next week."

The class scurried out, but Zaid and Zoya hung back, dragging their feet.

"Miss Ahmed ... please can you tell us more about the festival, and the stories, and the yellow and the food? Pleeeeease?" they begged.

"I am sorry, Zaid and Zoya, you will have to wait until next week, like the rest of the class," their teacher said kindly, nudging them out of the classroom door.

26

The twins walked home. They were met by their smiling father at the front of their house. They tossed their schoolbags to the ground and spoke over each other, getting louder and louder.

"Dad!"

"Tell us about the kite festival!"

"Dad!"

"What is Jashn-e-Baharan?"

Their father smiled and sat them down. "I think your dada might have some stories for you ..." So their grandfather joined them too.

Dada spoke quietly. "When your dad was a little boy, he would pray all year for the seasons to pass fast, so spring would arrive. We would take him to the markets and they would be filled with yellow scarves and kites of all sizes.

The streets were lined with stalls selling sweet things."

"My favourites were the biscuits and ladoos, so Mum would make them at home," Dad added.

"Yes, we would make our sweets at home and share them with our neighbours," Dada continued. "And we would wear our favourite yellow clothes and we would buy kites in all different shades of yellow. We flew those kites the night before spring was to arrive. The skies and street were yellow like the sun. We would celebrate for days and days at a time, until we could celebrate no more."

The children were confused. "But why don't we celebrate any more? Think of the fun we would have."

"Well, people got a bit greedy and competitive and started to see who could fly the biggest and highest kites. They fought so much that the skies became unsafe. Then, when the festival was over, the streets were lined with mess. It wasn't good for the people or the animals. So, slowly, people just stopped celebrating Jashn-e-Baharan."

Zaid and Zoya looked at each other with a grin. They knew exactly what the other was thinking.

"Perhaps we can celebrate again, Dada?" said Zoya.

"We promise we won't leave a mess behind ..." said Zaid.

The twins waited, just like their father had before them, for the seasons to pass. For the spring to come!

The night before spring arrived, they made ladoos and cherry biscuits with their dada, then they looked around for things in their house to make a kite with. They remembered Dada's story, so they didn't want to make something that flies in the sky then lands on the ground and makes a mess.

The Basant Kite Festival happens in January or February in India, and until recently, in Pakistan too. It celebrates the arrival of spring, when the yellow mustard flower blooms.

They found some old curtain rings in their garage and some yellow ribbon in Mum's sewing box. They tied the ribbon to the curtain rings and made little kites to hang from their trees in the front yard. These kites would never fall to the ground!

Then, while Zaid and Zoya stuffed their mouths with ladoos and biscuits, the kites swayed in the wind, the yellow ribbons flapping like sunbeams. Little yellow kites to welcome the spring.

PISTACHIO APRICOT LADOOS

Ladoos are treats that are made for many different festivals in Pakistan and India. Now you can make some at home for yourself. I've made mine with apricots, because of their beautiful bright colour, and pistachios for the crunch.

Makes 16

Ingredients

2 tbsp coconut oil

2 tbsp cashew butter or peanut butter

1 tbsp honey

pinch of salt

150g pistachios

100g dried apricots

grated zest of 1 lemon

Method

🐦 Put the coconut oil, cashew or peanut butter, honey and salt into a small saucepan and melt over a low heat, stirring until smooth. Set aside to cool.

🐦 Put the pistachios in a food processor and blitz until well crushed. Spoon 25g of them out into a bowl set on kitchen scales. Pour onto a plate and set aside, ready to coat the ladoos.

🐦 Now add the apricots and lemon zest to the remaining crushed pistachios in the food processor.

🐦 Pulse together and, as soon as the apricots have started to break down, add the cooled mixture from the pan.

🐦 Blend until the mixture comes together into a ball. Carefully remove the blade and put the mixture into a bowl.

🐦 Take tablespoons of mixture and roll and shape in your hands to create little balls.

🐦 Roll each ball in the crushed pistachios on the plate to coat evenly.

🐦 Cover and leave to chill and harden in the fridge. Take them out when you are ready to serve.

CHERRY BISCUITS

I love these biscuits because they have brightly coloured chewy cherries in them – and I do like a colourful biscuit! It's easy to find glacé cherries in red but they come in other colours too. You could use just one colour, or mix the colours together.

Makes 12

Ingredients

200g glacé cherries, any colour is fine

250g unsalted butter, softened

140g caster sugar

1 medium egg yolk

1 tsp almond extract

300g plain flour, plus extra for dusting

Method

- Rinse the cherries under cold water. This will help to get rid of the sticky syrup coating them.

- Put the cherries on some kitchen paper and pat them dry as well as you can. Now chop them into small pieces.

- Put the softened butter and sugar into a large bowl and mix until light and fluffy.

- Add the egg yolk and almond extract and give the mixture a quick stir.

- Add the cherries and mix them in well. Add the flour and, using a wooden spoon, bring the dough together as much as you can.

- Then, using floured hands, bring the dough together until smooth. Form it into a nice big ball, then flatten it slightly, wrap in cling film and pop into the fridge for 30 minutes.

- Line two large baking trays with some baking paper. Dust a work surface with flour and roll out the dough to a rectangle about 32 x 24cm and 1cm thick.

- Take a knife and cut the dough into 12 equal squares of about 8cm. Place each biscuit on a prepared tray and prick the surface with a fork.

- Chill in the freezer for 15 minutes, or in the fridge for 30 minutes. This will help the biscuits to keep their shape when they bake and stop them from spreading. Meanwhile, preheat the oven to 170°C fan/gas mark 5.

- Pop the biscuits into the oven for 18–25 minutes, or until the edges are crisp and the centre is just golden.

- Take out and leave to cool on the baking tray for 10 minutes, then carefully transfer to a cooling rack.

CURTAIN-RING KITES

You will need:

ribbon – you could use yellow for sunbeams, or lots of colours if you want to make a rainbow kite

scissors
curtain rings, or old costume bangles, or rings of loo roll
twine

To make:

Cut the ribbon into lengths with scissors. I like to use both long and short lengths.

Now tie each length of ribbon tightly around a ring. Use as many or as few ribbon lengths as you like.

Tie a piece of twine to the ring and use the twine to tie the kite on to the branch of a tree. You might need a grown-up's help for this, especially if you have to climb to get to the branch.

If you don't have a tree to tie it to, why not tie your kite to a door handle? Now you can have a beautiful kite hanging up all year round.

Holi

MUSHROOM SOUP FOR BREAKFAST

There was a quiet town in a quiet country in an even quieter part of the world. A large town with rows of streets, each one faultlessly lined up next to another. Perfectly parallel.

Each street had a name, and the first was called Grey Street. The next was called Greyer Street, the one next to that Even More Grey Street and so on. You get the idea.

The town's supermarkets only sold grey mushroom soup.

The schools only had grey crayons to draw with.

The cinema only showed grey films.

Everyone wore grey clothes and everyone's homes had grey walls.

But the people of the town didn't know anything different. They enjoyed their grey lives, with their grey colouring-in and their grey mushroom soup.

One day, a man called Ranj was driving through the town. He didn't mean to be there. He took a wrong turn and ended up in town by accident. But it was dark and he needed some food and a place to sleep for the night.

He found the town's hotel. He walked through the grey doors and checked in at the grey desk. He walked through the grey halls and into his grey room. He threw himself on his grey bed and ordered room service from the grey menu. He ordered mushroom soup, and then he went to sleep.

It was only when Ranj was at breakfast the next morning that he realised something wasn't quite right.

"Excuse me, miss," he said to his waitress. "Is this the right menu? Only ... there is only mushroom soup on here, and it's breakfast time."

"Yes, sir," the waitress replied, with the straightest face you ever did see. "We only do mushroom soup." And she walked away in her grey apron.

"Thank goodness I wore my grey clothes today," he said, quietly, "or I would have stuck out like a sore thumb."

After a soupy breakfast, Ranj checked out of the hotel and dragged his big suitcase out of the lobby. It was so heavy with all his work things. He dragged it down a grey kerb and SNAP! the whole case sprang open in a cloud of colour. For Ranj was a cook, and now all of his sprinkles and his spices and his cupcake cases were all over the pavement.

Everyone stopped and stared for a moment. The hotel manager rushed up to Ranj. "Are you okay there, sir? My eyes are hurting from all this ... all this ... er – what is this?" The manager swept his arms out wide, gesturing at the multicoloured pavement.

Ranj couldn't work out what the hotel manager was talking about, until he looked around at all the grey. "Colour!" he said. "It's colour! Surely you've seen colour before?"

The hotel manager shook his head, straightened his grey tie and went back inside, leaving Ranj to it. Ranj picked up his things and got into his car. *How can you live in a world with no colour?* he thought to himself.

A week later, Ranj came back to the quiet town with the same suitcase. This time, he was wearing his most colourful clothes and had covered his car in the brightest stickers he could find. He opened the boot of his car and pulled out some more suitcases that were full of goodies. He had made rainbow sprinkle fudge and golden hot chocolate spoons. In another case were bowls of red tomatoes and orange carrot sticks and fruit in all the beautiful jewel colours.

He put up a sign. It read: 'Come and try some colour, guaranteed to make you smile!'

But no one would come over to Ranj. They stood at a distance, squinting at him and his colourful car.

So Ranj reached into the back seat. He drew his hands back out, something in both fists. He opened his fingers and blew. POOOFFF! A cloud of red flour burst into the air. The people gasped. He opened his other fist. POOOFFF! A cloud of purple flour.

A little girl broke away from the crowd and ran over to Ranj. She tugged at his trousers. "It's magic!" she said. "Please can I try some colour?"

Ranj smiled down at the little girl and handed her a piece of rainbow fudge.

She looked at it, popped it into her mouth and smiled. Then a few more people came over. A mother, a grandmother, even a

puppy. Ranj brought out the boxes of
coloured flour he had on the back seat.
The people joyfully threw great handfuls
of the coloured flour in the air and all over
each other, laughing and shouting and filling
their mouths with Ranj's delicious, colourful food.

From that day on, the quiet grey town became a place of colour
and smiles. Mushroom soup was only served with a rainbow-
sprinkles topping and the people lived happily ever after in Red
Street, Orange Street, Yellow Street... You get the idea!

Holi is the festival of colours,
celebrated in February or
March by followers of the
Hindu, Sikh and Jain faiths.
Anyone can join in though, as
Holi unites people of all
backgrounds in
colourful joy!

RAINBOW FUDGE

Fudge can take quite a while to make, but it is worth the time!
Why not get some crayons and draw the most colourful picture
you can while you wait for it to set?

Makes 36 small squares

Ingredients

unsalted butter or vegetable oil, for the
  cake tin

450g milk chocolate, chopped

397g tin of condensed milk

1 tsp vanilla bean paste

50g rainbow sprinkles

Method

∿ Lightly butter or oil a 20cm square cake tin and line it with baking paper.

∿ Put the chocolate into a large saucepan with the condensed milk and vanilla bean paste.

∿ Over a low heat, mix it together until all the chocolate has melted and the mixture is smooth and one colour.

∿ Leave to simmer for about 3 minutes over a low heat, stirring occasionally.

∿ Pour into the tin and, using a palette knife, spread the fudge evenly to the edges. Then add the sprinkles evenly on top.

∿ Allow to cool, then pop into the fridge for at least 2 hours until set.

∿ Only cut into squares when the fudge is really firm.

GOLDEN HOT CHOCOLATE SPOONS

Colourful turmeric makes these chocolate spoons a perfect Holi present. If they are a gift to yourself, you can store them in a zip-lock bag in the fridge so they are ready for you to mix into hot milk when you fancy a golden hot chocolate.

Makes 10

Ingredients

50g white chocolate, broken into squares

50g white chocolate chips

½ tsp ground turmeric

½ tsp ground cinnamon

edible glitter stars, or sugar stars, or white chocolate stars

You will also need:

10 disposable wooden spoons, plus extra if needed

Method

- Arrange the spoons on a tray lined with baking paper.

- Put the white chocolate in a microwavable bowl and microwave for 1 minute. Stir, then microwave in 10-second bursts, stirring each time, until the chocolate is liquid.

- Once the chocolate is totally liquid, add the chocolate chips, turmeric and cinnamon and mix through until melted and smooth.

- Dip each spoon in the melted chocolate mixture and give it a good roll around to ensure it's evenly coated.

- If you have any mixture left, just prepare some extra spoons to use it up.

- Sprinkle each spoon with the stars, place back on the tray and leave to set in the fridge.

- When you are ready for a hot chocolate, warm some milk in a pan or in the microwave, pop in a chocolate spoon and keep stirring until your milk is golden and there is no more chocolate left on the spoon.

Nadiya's tip:
You could wrap up a couple of spoons in cellophane and give them to your friends as a sleepover present.

Easter

POOR OLD EASTER BUNNY

The Easter Bunny was in a bit of a jam. It was nearly Easter and it was her job to hide all the beautiful painted eggs for children to find. But there was a problem.

Her friends the hens were still tired from last Easter, and had decided that they needed a holiday. They'd gone off to a spa to get their feathers plumped and their beaks polished, so that meant there were no eggs for the Easter Bunny to decorate, or hide!

She hopped off into the forest to see if anyone could help.

"I'm sure I could find you some fir cones," said Owl.

"I'll share my acorns with you," offered Squirrel.

"I can raid some dustbins – there'll be treasure in there," said Fox.

But none of those things were quite right for the Easter Bunny, even though she was grateful that her friends wanted to help her.

She trudged home, and made herself a bowl of her favourite carrot and cumin soup.

The soup made the Easter Bunny feel much more lively, and she hopped about her kitchen, tidying up. One particularly large bounce dislodged a dusty recipe book on a high shelf, and the book fell at her feet. It was called *Chocolate for Bunnies*.

The Easter Bunny suddenly had a great idea ...

When Easter came, the bunny did her work, then tucked herself behind a bush to hide. A second later, a gang of children ran outside, empty baskets swinging from their arms, ready to collect the pretty painted eggs hidden in their garden. As the Easter Bunny watched, the first child squealed in delight and thrust his hand into a flowerpot.

Then he stopped and looked closer at what was in his palm. He sniffed it. Thought for a bit. Then he took a huge bite.

The Easter Bunny grinned to herself at the child's excitement. She had spent days and days making eggs out of chocolate, and luckily, the children liked them!

The Easter Bunny hopped all the way home and picked up her own basket from her kitchen. There was one more job to do. She bounced back to the forest and found her friends. The hens were back from the spa, looking very plumped and polished.

"Thank you for being lovely friends and offering to help me," she said to Owl, Squirrel and Fox, and she handed each of them their own

chocolate egg. "And hens, here's eggs for you, too. I'm sorry for making you tired."

From then on, a new tradition was born, and everyone always enjoyed a chocolate egg at Easter time.

Easter happens in March or April. It began as a celebration of new life in ancient times, with symbols like bunnies, and eggs, as we see at Easter now. Easter is also a festival for followers of the Christian faith.

CARROT AND CUMIN SOUP

Have a peek in your fridge. Are there are loads of carrots in the salad drawer? There always are in my fridge! Cooking them into a delicious soup is the perfect way to use them up. The Easter Bunny would definitely agree!

Serves 4

Ingredients

500g carrots

3 garlic cloves, peeled and crushed

250ml water

½ tsp salt

25g unsalted butter

800ml vegetable stock

1 tsp cumin seeds

large handful of baby spinach leaves

2 tbsp full-fat cream cheese

pepper

Nadiya's tip:
You can add a 1/2 teaspoon of ground cumin if you don't have cumin seeds.

Method

- Peel the carrots and take off the tops and the tips. Chop into 1cm-thick coins and place them in a large saucepan.

- Add the garlic, water, salt and butter to the pan. Put the lid on and leave to simmer over a medium heat for at least 25–30 minutes or until the carrots are soft and a knife goes right through them.

- Once the carrots are soft, add the stock and cumin seeds, let it come to the boil, then reduce the heat and leave to simmer for another 10 minutes.

- Now take the saucepan off the heat and add the spinach and cream cheese.

- Using a stick blender, whizz the soup until the carrots are puréed. Check the seasoning and add salt and pepper to taste.

EASTER EGG ROCKY ROAD

If you are not that confident yet about baking and need somewhere to start, this simple recipe is perfect for you. It's much more fun to put your Easter eggs into rocky road than it is to just gobble them all down in one go!

Makes 9 large squares, or 12 smaller rectangles

Ingredients

130g unsalted butter, plus extra for
   the tin

200g milk chocolate, chopped

3 tbsp golden syrup

200g digestive biscuits

150g sugar-coated mini chocolate
   eggs, roughly crushed in a food bag,
   plus 9–12 whole mini eggs for decorating

icing sugar, for dusting

Method

- Line and lightly butter a 20cm square cake tin, or a casserole dish about the same size.

- Put the butter, chocolate and golden syrup into a microwaveable bowl. Place in the microwave and microwave on high for 30 seconds. Take it out and mix. Put it back in the microwave for another 30 seconds and mix again. If it still hasn't completely melted, return it to the microwave for 10 seconds. When the mixture is glossy, runny and smooth, set aside to cool slightly.

- Put the biscuits and the 150g of mini eggs into a freezer bag and roughly crush with a rolling pin. They don't have to be as small and even as crumbs – they can be in small or larger pieces.

- Add the crushed biscuits and mini eggs to the melted mixture, then stir well until everything is covered with chocolate.

- Pour into the prepared tin or casserole dish and flatten with the back of a spoon.

- Add the whole mini eggs on top, equally spaced out according to how many pieces of rocky road you want to make, and gently push them in.

- Pop into the fridge to set for at least 2 hours.

- Once set, take it out and sift over icing sugar to dust. Cut into squares and enjoy!

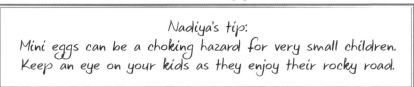

Nadiya's tip:
Mini eggs can be a choking hazard for very small children. Keep an eye on your kids as they enjoy their rocky road.

SOCK BUNNY

You will need:

a grown-up's sock (clean, of
  course!)

cotton wool, or scraps of old
  clothes or tights, to stuff

2 elastic bands

scissors

PVA glue

2 googly eyes

pink and white felt

a cotton-wool ball

ribbon of your choice

To make:

Stuff one-third of the sock with cotton wool, or scraps of clothes or tights, to make the body. Secure the top of the body with an elastic band.

Now add a bit less cotton wool or clothes into the sock above the elastic band, to make the head. Make sure you leave enough sock at the top to cut the ears.

Secure the top of the head with the other elastic band. Cut a vertical line down the middle of the remaining sock, all the way to the top of the elastic band. Carefully cut out ear shapes from both sides of the split.

Glue the googly eyes onto the head.

Cut out a little pink nose and two white teeth from the felt and glue them onto the bunny's face.

Now glue the cotton-wool ball on the back of the body, for the bunny's tail.

Tie the ribbon in a bow around the bunny's neck and give your new friend a name!

Family Day

DIG OUT YOUR WELLIES

Dad sat at the table, away with his thoughts,
He scrunched up his nose – his brain was up to all sorts.
He drank his black coffee and tapped the table top,
Then he got to his feet and cried, *"EVERYONE STOP!"*

Mum dropped her pen, she was slightly aghast,
The kids stopped their colouring and looked at Dad, fast.
The dog's ears pinged up – what was that sound?
Even the goldfish stopped swimming around.

Dad, he just stood there – he wouldn't sit down,
A beaming wide smile replacing his frown.
With hands behind back and chest puffed out high
He said, "Something is changing, and I'll tell you why."

There's Mother's Day for Mum and Father's Day for me,
But what about the day to celebrate you three?
We have birthdays to mark when you came along
But there's something else missing … My idea's not wrong!

What about a day when we stop what we do
To make it a day for you, you and you!
A day to stop working and care for each other,
A day where you celebrate – sister to brother.

So dig out your wellies, whack your sun cream on,

Let's get our scooters and scoot into the sun.

I'll pack a picnic, with all our best treats,

Devilled-egg sandwiches, sausage rolls and some sweets!

One day where we all show each other we care,

A day to give, to love, or simply to share.

And if you agree, then this much I can say,

I reckon we call it our 'Family Day'!

Families of all kinds are celebrated around the world on 15th May every year. This is the International Day of Families – so let's celebrate!

SAUSAGE ROLLS

Who doesn't love a sausage roll? I certainly do. These are extra-special, as they are cheesy! They taste great warm but are lovely when cold, too.

Makes 12

Ingredients

320g ready-rolled puff pastry

2 tbsp tomato ketchup

6 of your favourite kind of sausage

1 egg, lightly beaten

50g mature Cheddar cheese,
   finely grated

salt and pepper

Method

- Preheat the oven to 200°C fan/gas mark 7. Line a large baking tray with baking paper.

- Remove the pastry from its packaging and roll out so it's slightly thinner. Cut out 6 equal squares.

- Brush each square with some ketchup. Season with a little salt and pepper.

- Snip each end of each sausage and carefully peel the skin off, keeping the sausage shape.

- Pop a sausage onto a square of pastry, then roll it up in its pastry blanket. Brush the end of the pastry with a little beaten egg and press the seam down.

- Using scissors or a knife, cut the roll in half. Pop both rolls on the prepared tray. Repeat to form the rest of the sausage rolls.

- Cut a couple of slashes in the top of each roll, then brush with more of the egg.

- Sprinkle with the cheese and bake for 20–25 minutes.

Nadiya's tip:
You can replace meat sausages with veggie ones if you like. There's not usually skin to remove from vegetarian sausages, so just skip that stage in the method.

DEVILLED-EGG SANDWICHES

Devilled eggs are fancy eggs that grown-ups eat at parties. But I think they are much tastier in between soft slices of brown bread and perfect to take on a family day out.

Makes 24 small triangles

Ingredients

8 medium eggs

3 tbsp mayonnaise

2 tbsp salad cream

½ tsp paprika

large handful of chives, chopped

12 slices of brown bread

salted butter, for spreading

salt and pepper

Method

🐚 Bring a large saucepan of water to the boil over a high heat, carefully lower in each egg on a spoon, then return to the boil for 8 minutes.

🐚 Empty the saucepan into a washing-up bowl filled with cold water and leave the eggs to cool.

🐚 Peel the boiled eggs and cut them in half. Remove all the yolks and pop them into a bowl.

🐚 Slice the egg whites and put them into another bowl.

🐚 Crush the egg yolks using the back of a fork. Add the mayonnaise, salad cream, paprika and chives and mix to a smooth paste. Season to taste with salt and pepper.

🐚 Lay out the slices of bread in pairs for sandwiching. Butter both slices, I like to be generous!

🐚 Now spread some of the egg yolk mixture on one half of the slices, dividing the mixture equally between the six slices of bread.

🐚 Add the slices of egg white on top and put the remaining slices of bread on top of that.

🐚 Cut into triangles and put on a plate if you're eating at home, or pop into some sandwich bags if you're taking them out.

NOT VICTORIA'S SANDWICH

Ever wondered why this famous treat is called a 'sandwich' when, actually, it's a cake? I'm not sure either ... I bet that Victoria would love my version of her cake even more than the original, as it has a yummy banana flavour.

Serves 8-10

Ingredients

225g unsalted butter, softened, plus extra for the tins

225g caster sugar

4 medium eggs, lightly beaten

2 tbsp whole milk

225g self-raising flour, sifted

2 tsp baking powder

150ml whipping cream

2 tbsp banana milkshake powder

50g banana chips, crushed

icing sugar, for dusting

Method

Preheat the oven to 160°C fan/gas mark 4. Lightly butter two 20cm sandwich tins and line the bases with baking paper.

Put the butter, sugar, eggs, milk, flour and baking powder in a large mixing bowl and mix with an electric whisk or a wooden spoon for a few minutes. The mixture should be light and fluffy.

Divide the mixture equally between the tins and level off the tops.

Bake in the oven for 25 minutes, until the sponge is golden. A skewer inserted into the centre of the cakes should come out clean.

Take out and leave to cool in the tin for 10 minutes before turning out onto a wire rack.

Once the sponge is totally cold, prepare the filling.

Put the cream and milkshake powder into a bowl and whip until you have soft peaks. Add the banana chips and fold through.

Pile the cream on the top of one of the sponges and sandwich the other sponge on top.

Sift over a little icing sugar, cut a slice and enjoy. This is not Victoria's, this is yours!

HAND HEART CARD

You will need:

coloured card

a pen

your hand

scissors

glitter, stickers or felt-tip pens
  (all optional)

To make:

Fold a piece of card in half, with the fold on your right-hand side.

Take your left hand and place it flat on the card, with the thumb and index finger (your pointing finger) just touching and overlapping the fold.

Draw around your hand, all the way up to your wrist.

Cut out your hand shape, being careful not to cut through the fold.

Open up the card and you should have what looks like two hands joining to make a heart shape.

You could decorate it with glitter, or stickers, or felt-tip pens. Then write a message inside and give your hand heart card to someone special.

Nadiya's tip:
If you are left-handed, make sure the fold in the card is on the left-hand side and that you draw around your right hand!

Eid

THE BEST
PRESENT OF ALL

It was the night before the month of Ramadan. My mum piled me, my sister and my brothers into a hug and said, "Ramadan Mubarak my little ones." It was a great tight doughnut of a hug.

"What is Ramadan?" said my baby sister Leeya. But before Mum could answer, keys jingled in the door.

"Baba's home!" we all cried.

"Home early today. Let's get ready for Ramadan!" Dad exclaimed, coming through the door and throwing his arms up into the air in greeting.

Suddenly everything sped up like life was on fast forward. Dad rushed around and got us all ready for bed. We washed and bathed and moisturised. We brushed our teeth. We read our books, then Dad read us more of our books.

Meanwhile downstairs, Mum was making quite a commotion, cleaning the kitchen, tidying up and preparing food. Then we all snuggled in Mum and Dad's bed, under the covers, and we spoke about Ramadan. The same thing we did every year, but now, baby Leeya was old enough to understand.

Mum started, like she always did. "Ramadan is the ninth month in the Islamic Calendar. Your dad and I fast for the thirty days of this month. So that means no eating or drinking from the time between sunrise and sunset. But we can—"

"You can eat the rest of the time!" My brother Deen loved to butt in and finish off the story.

"Thanks, Deen," Dad said with a wink. "Now, do you remember what comes next? In these thirty days, we will give up food and spend more time praying, spend more time with each other, giving more charity and taking life a little slower."

"Tell us about the best bit, Dad, the bit about after we sight the moon," I said.

Dad smiled at me. "Of course, Maya – how could I forget your favourite bit ... Well, when we get to the end of our thirty days, we wait for the full moon, and then when it is sighted–"

"We have our meal at sunset and celebrate Eid with food and prayers and presents the next day!" I shouted, at the same time as Deen and my other brother, Zakaria.

We all jumped up, out from under the covers, sending the bedding flying, and chattering about all the food we would eat at Eid.

"Whoop! Mum's date biscuits!" Deen said.

"Dad's saffron rice," said Zakaria as he hung from Dad's neck.

Leeya clapped her hands in delight.

Mum and Dad looked at each other.

"So, how do we get these over-excited kids to bed, now?" Mum sighed.

With my brothers and baby sister, I counted down the days to Eid. Day one, day eight, day fourteen, day twenty-two …

Mum and Dad would wake in the dark night to make our breakfast.

Then wake again to take us to school.

They went to work all day. Picked us up. Took us to swimming, to karate, to ballet, then they came home and made us our dinner, all with no food in their belly and no water to quench their thirst.

I loved my mum and dad for that, and spent a lot of time wondering what we could do to show them how much we loved them.

All of a sudden, it was day twenty-nine. The night before Eid! We knew we would get presents the next day, but there was only one thing on my mind … I didn't even care that much about seeing the beautiful full moon! I gathered my brothers and sister while Mum and Dad were busy loading the dishwasher and whispering to each other (about presents, Deen was sure). We made a plan and then went to sleep.

Very early the next morning, my alarm went off. I went to each bedroom and woke up my siblings, one by one. We made sure we avoided the creaky step going downstairs and quietly shut the kitchen door behind us.

We knew that Mum and Dad would have started preparations for Eid. Our plan was to finish it all off before they came down!

Hours later, Mum and Dad found the four of us fast asleep at the dining table. The jewelled saffron rice was ready and the almond crescents were waiting to be baked. We had made them so

many times with Mum, we knew exactly what we were doing.

Mum scooped us all into another of her doughnut hugs. "You sacrificed your sleep to help us, my little ones," she said, and squeezed us tight. "You are the best Eid present of all."

SAFFRON JEWELLED RICE

The best kind of jewels are the kind you can eat. This dish dazzles with glowing red cranberries and green pistachios, plus saffron gives the rice a beautiful yellow colour. In my family, we love to make this for special celebrations, but you can also make it for your tea any time you want.

Makes 12

Ingredients

50g unsalted butter

1 large cinnamon stick, snapped in half

1 red onion, finely chopped

1 tsp salt

300g basmati rice, rinsed in a sieve

25g dried cranberries

25g pistachios, kept whole

large pinch of saffron threads

700ml hot water

Method

- Put a medium non-stick saucepan over a medium heat.

- Add the butter and the cinnamon stick and allow the cinnamon to infuse into the butter. You should be able to smell it in the air.

- Now add the onion and salt and cook the onion until soft. This should take about 5 minutes.

- Add the rice, cranberries, pistachios and saffron and cook in the butter for about 5 minutes. Make sure you stir all the time - the rice should look glossy.

- Now pour in the hot water and increase the heat. Make sure to stir the pan occasionally so the rice doesn't get a chance to settle and stick to the bottom.

- Allow rice to boil and the liquid to evaporate completely.

- Once all the liquid has evaporated, reduce the heat to the lowest possible. Put a secure lid on top and leave to steam for 15 minutes.

- Fluff up the rice with a fork and get ready to eat!

DATE-AND-ORANGE CRESCENTS

It's always fun to work with dough, and, luckily, these delicious biscuits need plenty of squishing and rolling and shaping. The sweet date-and-orange filling will be a tasty surprise when you bite in!

Makes 30

Ingredients

For the date-and-orange filling

225g dates, pitted

2 tbsp hot water

pinch of salt

grated zest of 1 orange

For the biscuit dough

115g unsalted butter, softened

25g caster sugar

pinch of salt

60ml whole milk

280g plain flour, plus extra for dusting

icing sugar, for dusting

Method

- Make the filling by putting the dates, water, salt and orange zest in a blender and blitzing the mixture to a thick paste. Scrape into a bowl and set aside.

- To make the dough, put the butter and sugar in a large bowl and whisk with an electric whisk, or beat with a wooden spoon until the mixture is light, pale and fluffy.

- Add the salt, milk and flour and bring together, first using a pallet knife and then – just get your hands in!

- Line two baking trays with baking paper. Preheat the oven to 140°C fan/gas mark 3.

- Dust a work surface with flour, then roll the dough out into a sausage shape and cut into 30 equal pieces.

- Take one piece of dough and flatten it in your hands. Dollop 1 small teaspoon of the filling in the centre and wrap the dough around the filling to cover it all up, forming it into an oval shape.

- To make the crescent-moon shape, tease both ends of the oval towards each other, then flatten the dough slightly using the back of your hand.

- Put the crescent on a prepared baking tray and repeat with the rest of the pieces of dough and filling.

- Pop into the oven and bake for 25 minutes, until golden. Leave to cool completely on the tray.

- Sift over icing sugar before serving.

Nadiya's tip:
Why not make your crescents extra special by showering them with edible glitter? That's exactly what I do with mine for Eid!

International Friendship Day
THE RAINBOW WORLD

There was another world, in another galaxy, that was round. Parts of it were land. But mostly it was water.

A lot of different things lived in this world, but they kept themselves to themselves in their own little places.

The red birds had their own place. In another place were the oranges. The yellow pencils were next door to the oranges. On the other shore of the sea were the broccoli. A hundred miles from them were the blue slippers. And on the far side of the world were the pink unicorns, who lived not too far from the purple bodybuilders. The purple bodybuilders didn't much like the unicorns and their pink sparkle, but it was okay – they just avoided each other.

One day, when they were all just going about their business, there was a tremble in the ground. It went away for second and then it came back. Then it came back again, but this time it was a huge RUMBLE.

The rumble was so big and so strong that it jumbled the world up. When everyone opened their eyes, it was like a rainbow had spilled over. They were all mixed up.

The red birds were confused. The yellow pencils couldn't work out what was going on. And the pink unicorns just stamped their feet and tossed their glittery manes in bewilderment. They all preferred being in their own little places, but they knew that they had to keep going until they could find a way of restoring things to how they used to be.

So everyone got together and made food to share. They made monkey bread and a huge pot of chocolate fondue. Then they sat down and made friendship bracelets for one another, using all the colours around them.

As their jumbled-up, mixed-together day came to an end, everyone realised they quite liked their new rainbow world. But, suddenly, there was another tremble. And then a rumble. They held on tight and closed their eyes. When they opened them again, the yellow pencils were all together, the blue slippers the same, so were the broccoli, and all the others too – all back in their own places. No more rainbow world.

But they were still wearing their friendship bracelets.

So the red birds, the oranges, the yellow pencils, the broccoli, the blue slippers, the pink unicorns and the purple bodybuilders agreed to get mixed up once a year. Rainbow Day became the best day of the year for these new friends.

On July 30th all over the world, people celebrate the International Day of Friendship. It is a day for finding out about each other and building peace between us.

MONKEY BREAD

This recipe needs a sprinkling of patience, but it's worth it because when it is finished, you get to share it with your friends and family. And sharing is definitely the best part of eating!

Serves 12–14

Ingredients

For the bread

200ml whole milk

85g unsalted butter, plus extra for the tin

2 medium eggs, lightly beaten

550g self-raising flour, plus extra for
  dusting

2½ tsp fast-action dried yeast

40g caster sugar

For the coating

125g unsalted butter, melted

200g caster sugar

3 tbsp cocoa powder

To decorate

100g chocolate spread

25g roasted hazelnuts, chopped

You will also need

25cm bundt tin

Method

✱ Put the milk and butter in a pan and gently warm till the butter has melted completely. Then allow to cool.

✱ Once cooled, add the eggs to the pan and mix through.

✱ Put the flour, yeast and sugar in a large mixing bowl and mix it all together. Make a well in the centre of the mixture.

✱ Pour the wet ingredients into the well and, using a palette knife, bring the dough together. Then get your hands in and form a large lump of dough.

✱ On a lightly floured work surface, knead for 10 minutes till the dough is smooth. Or do it by machine, in a food mixer fitted with a dough hook, for 5–10 minutes.

✱ Pop the dough into a lightly oiled bowl and cover with cling film. Put it in a warm place and let it double in size. This will take around 1 hour.

✱ Meanwhile, thoroughly grease the inside of a 25cm bundt tin with butter.

✱ After 1 hour, flatten the dough to knock out the air. Pinch a piece of the dough, about the size of a golf ball, and shape it into a small ball. You'll need to make about 60 balls in total.

✱ Now you need to coat the dough balls. Place the melted butter, sugar and cocoa into three separate bowls.

✱ Take each ball of dough and dip it into the butter, then roll it in the sugar and finally in the cocoa, then put it into the bundt tin. You don't have to be neat, just fill up that tin, making sure all the balls are touching each other.

✱ Cover again with cling film and leave for another hour. Preheat the oven to 160°C fan/gas mark 4.

✱ Remove the cling film and bake the bread for 35 minutes. Leave in the tin for 30 minutes, until just warm, before turning out.

✱ Decorate by melting the chocolate spread in the microwave for 30 seconds, then drizzle it over the monkey bread and sprinkle the hazelnuts over the top. (You can also pipe on the chocolate spread without melting it, if you feel like being fancy.)

✱ Enjoy tearing and sharing!

CHOCOLATE FONDUE

Chocolate fondue doesn't have to be saved for special occasions or parties. With this recipe, you can have it at home on any old day, with all your favourite things to dip in.

Serves 4-6

Ingredients

For the things to dip

1 mango

large punnet of strawberries

large bowl of crunchy salted pretzels

mini doughnuts

100g dried apricots

150g marshmallows

For the sprinkles

50g rainbow sprinkles

50g chopped nuts

50g desiccated coconut

50g crushed biscuits

For the fondue

300g milk chocolate

300ml double cream

You will also need

cocktail sticks

Nadiya's tip:
If the chocolate starts to get too thick, all you need to do is pop it into a microwaveable bowl and microwave for 10 seconds to make it a bit more liquid again.

Method

- Start by preparing all the fruit. Peel the mango, remove the stone and cut it into slices. Remove the hull (the white inner bit) from the strawberries and cut any larger strawberries in half.

- Arrange on a large platter with all the other things to dip, leaving a big space in the centre where the bowl of chocolate will go.

- Next prepare the sprinkles. Pour each type of sprinkle into separate small bowls and pop them on the side.

- Break the chocolate into pieces and place into a large heatproof bowl.

- Pour the cream into a pan and heat to just-before-boiling (it should be steaming, but not bubbling), then take it off the heat.

- Pour the cream over the chocolate immediately and give the mixture a stir. Keep stirring until really smooth.

- Pour into a serving bowl and put into the centre of the platter.

- Dip your fruit, pretzels, doughnuts, apricot or marshmallows into the chocolate, then dip into the sprinkles of your choice. Yum!

FRIENDSHIP BRACELET

You will need:

colourful cardboard straws

thick string or wool

scissors

To make:

Take lots of cardboard straws and cut them into 1cm lengths to form stubby cylinders. The more colourful the better!

Take some thick string or wool and measure the size of your wrist. Cut the string to the correct size, leaving plenty of room both to get your hand through and to tie up the ends.

String a selection of the straw cylinders onto the string or wool. You can follow a colour pattern or go for a random order.

Once you have enough straws on your bracelet, get a friend to help you tie the ends of the string or wool in a bow. Don't forget to take off your bracelet at bath time!

Thanksgiving
MR PLYMOUTH ROCK

Let me introduce myself.

My name is Plymouth. Mr Plymouth Rock. And I live in the United States of America. Are you comfortable? Let me tell you a story.

Once upon a very long time ago (and when I say long time, we're talking the year 1620 – that is a very, very, VERY long time ago. Way back further than your parents, your parents' parents, your parents' parents' parents … It was a long time ago.) Anyway, it was just an ordinary day and I was doing what all rocks do. Nothing.

Then suddenly, CRASH! A huge boat smacked right into me. It was the loudest sound I had ever heard. Good job rocks don't feel anything, I can tell you! This boat had its name written on the side. It was called the Mayflower. Out came two men, both smartly dressed.

"What do we have here?" one said, curious, looking at me.

"Maybe this is it. Perhaps this is the place we can call home?"

"Well, if we are calling this home, home has to have a name." There was a short pause. "I think we will call it Plymouth. It'll remind us of Plymouth in England, where we set sail from."

"I think we should name this rock too," the other man said. "After all, if we hadn't crashed into it we may never have stopped to get out. It's a sure sign."

"Let's call it Plymouth Rock, then!" said the first man. "Fantastic idea."

So they got off their boat and behind them followed a crowd of people. There were men, women and children, some dogs, pigs and chickens. They all looked pretty tired and a bit green. The sea was pretty choppy that day.

They got to work setting up their homes, digging, building, hammering and sawing. They even fixed a hole in the boat.

I never did understand why they moved here in winter. It was very, very, VERY cold.

There was no food. They had shelter, but nothing to eat.

"Whose idea was it to move?"

"We should have just stayed where we were!"

The people shouted at one another. They were cold, and so hungry. I wished I could do something to help, but – hey, I'm just a rock.

The people managed through winter with the warmth of hope in their hearts to carry them through. As soon as the first grass shoot peeked through, they ploughed the ground and planted their first seeds. It was beginning to feel like home.

One day some local people came to visit. "We didn't know we had neighbours," said one startled local.

The new people welcomed their new neighbours.

"We heard that you have moved in and we wanted to welcome you. We wanted to get you a present, but we couldn't find any good candles or plants, so we got you a turkey ... Do you like turkey?"

In October or November, people across Canada and the United States gather to celebrate **Thanksgiving Day**. This harvest festival marks the time when, in 1621, English immigrants and Native American Wampanoag feasted together.

Like turkey? They loved turkey!

The neighbours worked hard together to make this the best harvest they had ever had. It really was the most abundant they had ever seen. Especially because they worked together. To celebrate, they shared their food and had a great big feast.

So every year they did the same thing. They shared their harvest with turkey and all the things they were thankful for. Especially the day they bumped into me.

I am still here today … if you ever want to visit.

ROCK CAKES

You can pretend you are actually eating rocks when you dig into these delicious little cakes! Thankfully they don't taste like real rocks ... Enjoy them dipped in a cup of something warm, or just eat them straight from the baking tray once they have cooled a little.

Makes 12

Ingredients

125g unsalted butter, cut into cubes, plus extra for the trays

225g self-raising flour, sifted

75g soft brown sugar

1 tsp baking powder

seeds from 2 cardamom pods, crushed

100g dried cranberries

50g white chocolate chips

1 large egg

1 tbsp whole milk

Nadiya's tip:
If you want to make these extra-special you could melt 50g white chocolate (see page 131) and pop it into a piping bag, or a freezer bag with the tip snipped off. Drizzle the chocolate all over your cooled rock cakes.

Method

- Preheat the oven to 160°C fan/gas mark 4. Lightly butter two large baking trays and line them with baking paper.

- In a large bowl, rub the butter and flour together until it looks like fine breadcrumbs, then stir in the sugar, baking powder and crushed cardamom seeds.

- Now add the dried cranberries and white chocolate chips and mix them in well.

- In a smaller bowl, beat the egg with the milk until combined.

- Make a well in the centre of the dry ingredients and add all the wet ingredients. Using a pallet knife, thoroughly mix together until there are no more dry, floury bits.

- Now spoon out dollops of the mixture the size of large golf balls and plop on to one of the prepared trays. Use another spoon to help push them off. Make 6 dollops on each tray and leave some space between each cake.

- Bake in the oven for 18–20 minutes until golden brown.

- Now you have to be patient and let the rock cakes cool for at least 10 minutes on the trays. Then you can enjoy!

TURKEY KEBABS

This is such a great recipe for getting your hands messy. The kebabs are delicious dunked in the dip or you could pop it all into some pittas together. The paprika gives them a wonderful smoky flavour.

Makes 12

Ingredients

For the kebabs

500g minced turkey

½ tsp smoked paprika

½ tsp garlic granules

2 tsp dried parsley

½ tsp salt

1 small egg, lightly beaten

55g dried breadcrumbs

oil spray, or a little vegetable oil

For the dip

150g tomato ketchup

1 tsp smoked paprika

large handful of chives, chopped

Method

- Preheat the oven to 200°C fan/gas mark 7.

- Pop the minced turkey into a large bowl. Add the paprika, garlic, parsley and salt, then get your hands in and give it all a good mix.

- Now add the egg and mix again.

- Add the breadcrumbs and mix for a final time. Lots of mixing will mean all the flavours will spread evenly.

- Take a small handful of the mixture, about the size of a golf ball, and form it into a sausage shape. Put it on a baking tray, then spray or lightly brush the top of the kebab with oil.

- Bake for 15 minutes, making sure to turn the kebabs halfway through cooking.

- Meanwhile, make the dip by mixing the ketchup, smoked paprika and chives in a bowl.

- Serve the kebabs warm and dip away!

THANKSGIVING WREATH

You will need:

large, clean leaves

marker pen

2 sheets of A4 card

To make:

Collect the biggest, cleanest leaves you can find, checking for any little critters on them. The leaves will be golden at Thanksgiving time, but you can make the wreath at any time of year!

Think about what you are thankful for. What makes you feel warm and fuzzy inside? It could be your pets, your friends – even just your snuggly bed. Mine are my kids and my welly socks.

Now take a marker pen and write something you are thankful for on each leaf.

Take two pieces of A4 card and tape them together along one of the long edges.

Cut out as big a circle as you can and a smaller circle inside that to form a ring, making sure it's quite a thick ring so you've got enough room to stick down your leaves. You might need to get a grown-up to help.

Now take your leaves and stick them onto the ring of card.

Leave the glue to dry and you will have a beautiful wreath to hang on your door or use as a centrepiece on your Thanksgiving dinner table.

Nadiya's tip:
Why not ask other people in your home if they'd like to join in.
You could go out together to find leaves and then take it in turns
writing something on each leaf.

Halloween
JACK O AND JACKIE

Jack Otto and Jackie were friends. Or, rather, they were frenemies. Sometimes they liked each other, but the rest of the time they loathed one another. Jackie called him Jack O because she knew it drove him mad.

Jack O was mischievous and rather selfish. He didn't worry much about anyone but himself. Not even Jackie. He laughed at his own jokes and made jokes about others.

One afternoon the pair were playing by Jackie's dad's tiny pumpkin patch. Jackie loved hanging out down here, because her favourite colour was orange and her favourite biscuits to eat were pumpkin flavour – her dad made special pumpkin-shaped window biscuits just for her to bring down to the patch. She even wore pumpkin-shaped earrings every day. And you guessed it – Halloween was her favourite time of year! Jackie wanted to look after the patch herself when she grew up, and just like her dad, she wanted to be the best pumpkin grower in the village. She went into a daydream … until she was rudely interrupted!

"Oh, look, there's a pumpkin growing in that tree up there!" yelled Jack O.

"Don't be daft," Jackie yelled back. "Pumpkins DO NOT grow in trees."

But Jack O would not shut up. He kept hollering about a pumpkin in a tree. So Jackie ran over to the tree and without thinking twice, she dropped her biscuit to the ground, yanked up her dress and started to climb.

Now, Jackie and Jack O were master tree climbers. Mainly because they would compete with each other to climb the quickest. But today she was slipping and sliding all over the place. She looked at her hands. Slime.

Aha, this slime has Jack O written all over it, she thought. I'll show him. And she slipped and slid her way slowly to the top. No pumpkin.

"There's no pumpkin here. You tricked me again!" she called down. All of a sudden, she realised how high she had climbed. Her knees wobbled, and her toes tingled and she felt sick.

She realised that, for the first time ever, she was afraid of heights!

Jack O just laughed. "*Ha-ha, made you look,*" he teased and ran away.

Unlucky for Jack O, Jackie always told her mum everything. After closing her eyes and being really brave, she got herself down from the tree, ran home and that is exactly what she did. She told her mum.

Jackie was not allowed to play with Jack O any more. Her mum reminded her she was a kind girl and not everyone, especially Jack O, could appreciate that.

Jackie didn't miss Jack O, not that much. She made new friends, friends who loved the pumpkin patch as much as she did. Jack O never made another frenemy after Jackie, just enemies. Nobody liked him.

Eventually Jack O moved away. His dad had opened a dog-food tasting company in the city. Jack O was gone and not a soul missed him.

Years went by, and as Jackie grew, so did her pumpkin patch. Her dad had died when Jackie was a teenager, and Jackie remembered her dad with each pumpkin flower that blossomed.

Every day, Jackie would sit on the side of the patch,

looking through a pumpkin window biscuit and thinking about things. One day, she found herself wondering what had happened to Jack O ...

Deep in the city, Jack O was miserable. He thought about Jackie a lot. He had never made any friends after he moved to the big city. Nobody hung around long enough to find any of his jokes funny. Everyone was too busy. Plus, it's not that easy making friends when your breath smells like dog food.

One day, Jack O plucked up the courage to tell his dad, "Dad, the dog-food tasting business is just not for me."

There was a long pause. "It's your lucky day, Jack Otto, I was going to fire you anyway. You are my son, but the staff just cannot work with you, you are too rude. It's business, you understand?"

Jack O, not in the least bit upset, walked out through the revolving doors and headed straight for a special pumpkin patch in a village he had not seen in forever.

The pumpkin patch was bright orange from all the pumpkins ready for Halloween. The old tree where he last played with Jackie was still standing tall, and there, crouching in the soil, was a young woman. He recognised her instantly and tapped her on her shoulder.

"Hi, I was hoping to get a job on the patch," he said.

"There are no vacancies, I'm very sorry," she said, without turning round.

"Not even for an old frenemy?"

Jackie went very still, frozen at the familiar voice. But when she finally turned around, he had already disappeared.

Typical Jack O, she thought. She had hoped he had changed over the years but he had not changed one bit. He was still playing tricks at other people's expense. She sighed and carried on tending to the pumpkin patch.

The next morning, Jackie woke up to a delivery. It was the biggest box she had ever received. Inside were hundreds of biscuits, all sandwiched together with sprinkles inside.

There was a note attached:

"I would like to think that perhaps once we were friends and not frenemies. Share these pumpkin biscuits, shine a torch through them, shake them, smile and have a Happy Halloween."

Jackie picked up one of the biscuits and gave it a shake. The rattling sound it made put a big smile on her face.

"Thanks, Jack Otto," she whispered.

Jackie never saw Jack O again. But every Halloween she would make pumpkin biscuits and give them to children far and wide, so everyone could enjoy what Jack O left behind, and Jackie could remember Jack O, her friend.

To: The Pumpkin PATch.

PUMPKIN RATTLE
BISCUITS

These spiced biscuits are so much fun – they're a toy and a snack all in one! If you prefer, you can make a simpler version with the little sweetie window to peek through, without sandwiching them together.

24 single biscuits, or 12 sandwiched biscuits

Ingredients

100g unsalted butter, softened

100g caster sugar

1 medium egg

275g self-raising flour, sieved, plus
  extra for dusting.

2 tsp mixed spice

For the decorations

18 boiled sweets, any colour you like

50g milk chocolate, melted (see
  page 131)

small sprinkles of your choice

You will also need

7 x 7.5cm pumpkin-shaped cutter

3.5cm round cutter

116

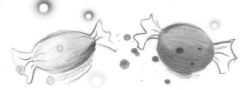

Method

- Beat the butter and sugar until light and fluffy. Add the egg and mix it in really well.

- Add the flour and mixed spice to a separate bowl, mix, then add to the wet mixture.

- Use a palette knife to bring the dough together, then get your hands in and bring into a big lump.

- Flatten the dough a little, wrap in cling film and leave to chill in the fridge for 30 minutes. Line two baking trays with baking paper and butter them lightly.

- Dust a work surface with flour. Roll out the dough to about 5mm thick. Using the pumpkin-shaped cutter, cut out as many pumpkins as you can. Pop these onto one of the prepared trays.

- Using the round cutter, cut out a circle inside of each pumpkin. This is the space where you will create the sweetie window.

- Gather the scraps of dough, bring them together and roll out again. Cut out more pumpkin shapes and add them to the trays. Repeat until you have 24 biscuits.

- Put the tray in the fridge to chill the dough for 10–15 minutes. Meanwhile, preheat the oven to 170°C fan/gas mark 5.

- Bake the biscuits in the oven for 10 minutes.

- Meanwhile, crush the sweets using a pestle and mortar, or by putting them in a strong zip-lock bag and crushing them with the end of a rolling pin. Try and crush them as evenly as you can.

- Take the biscuits out of the oven and spoon the crushed sweets into each of the holes. Make sure to divide the crushed sweets equally between the 24 biscuits.

- Now pop the trays back in the oven for another 6 minutes until all the sweets have dissolved and formed a smooth 'window'.

- When you take them out of the oven, don't touch them until they are totally cool.

- To make the sandwiched rattle biscuits, put the melted chocolate in a piping bag and pipe around the outer edge of half the biscuits, making sure the flat side of each biscuit is facing upwards.

- Spoon ½ teaspoon of sprinkles on to each sweetie window of the biscuits with the chocolate on and sandwich with another, non-chocolatey biscuit, this time flat side down. (The flat sides of both biscuits should be stuck together.)

- Let the chocolate set and they are ready to shake and eat.

EDIBLE SLIME

You could serve this oozy, squidgy dough to a friend or sibling as a Halloween joke. With clean hands, squish and prod it before you take a little bite – why not close your eyes and imagine what it feels like ... A monster's tummy? Or a ghost's slime?

Makes enough for a playdate!

Ingredients

6 white medium-sized marshmallows

6 tsp water

6 tsp vegetable oil, plus more for your hands

1 drop green food colouring

1 drop peppermint extract

1 tsp edible glitter

30 tbsp (about 280g) icing sugar, sifted

Method

🦇 Put the marshmallows and water into a large microwavable bowl. Melt on high for 30 seconds. Take out and mix until you have removed most of the lumps.

🦇 Add the oil and mix again, then add the food colouring, peppermint extract and edible glitter.

🦇 Now add 1 tablespoon of icing sugar and mix until the sugar disappears. Add the rest of the sugar 1 tablespoon at a time, mixing after each tablespoon is added.

🦇 Rub a little oil on your hands and bring the dough together.

🦇 Now you can play with it, or if you can't wait ... just eat that slime!

GHOSTLY POTATO PRINTS

You will need:

pencil

paper

1 large potato

1 knife

saucer or paper plate

paint

plain paper or card

To make:

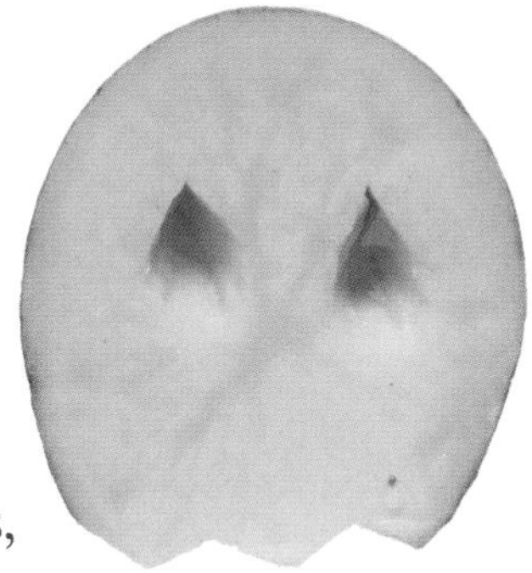

Draw a spooky face on a piece of paper. You could draw a ghost or maybe a scary pumpkin, like I have.

Ask a grown-up to cut a potato in half lengthways, then ask them to copy your spooky drawing onto the flat side of the potato and carve it in with a knife.

Take the potato and dip the flat side into a saucer or paper plate of paint, so your spooky face is covered.

Print it onto some paper or card.

You could make a Halloween card, or some invites to a Halloween party, or even a scary potato-print poster to put up on the wall!

There was a family that lived at 30 Ashbrook Grove. They were not your ordinary family. They were very, VERY different.

There was Alfred the Great Dane and the love of his life, Hira the Persian Grey. Then there were their roommates, August the hamster, whose room was next to Dave the snake's. Mabel the giant bunny lived in the kitchen.

This weird and wonderful family were lucky. They had butlers who looked after them – the Joneses. The Joneses were the best butlers around.

The Joneses worked hard for their family. They fed them. They groomed them. They cleaned up after them. They even accompanied them on their exercise. The butlers made sure the family wanted for nothing.

"Darling, we are sooooo lucky," Hira purred to Alfred. "You know the family three doors down? The budgies? They only have one butler. Between eight of them!"

The only problem the family had was that they couldn't communicate with their butlers. They tried, but no matter how much they barked and miaowed and squeaked and hissed, the Joneses just couldn't understand.

One day, the family were lounging about after the butlers had served lunch. *Loose Women* was on the telly and today's topic was: "Petrified pets! How do we help our animal friends with Bonfire Night approaching?"

Alfred the Great Dane's ears pinged up. "Bonfire Night? It can't be Bonfire Night again so soon! I've only just recovered from the last one!"

He started to panic and paced up and down the lounge, nearly knocking August's cage to the ground.

"Calm down, Alfie," August said in a soothing voice through the cage bars.

"I LOVE fireworks," said Dave the snake.

"Shhhhh," they all said.

"Sssssss," said Dave.

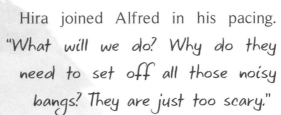

Hira joined Alfred in his pacing. "What will we do? Why do they need to set off all those noisy bangs? They are just too scary."

Mabel came out from under a cushion. "Look, the Loose Women said that we need to create a den, so that's what we'll do. We can just stay there for the night."

"Excellent plan, Mabel," said August. "But don't forget to press record on the tv before we start. You know how the butlers love to watch Loose Women when they come home from whatever it is they do when they're not waiting on us."

While Mabel sorted out the recording, Albert and Hira popped through the dog flap and made a dash for the garage. They needed supplies like extra sheets and sticks to build the den.

Inside the garage, they found Ru the rat huddled up with Ali the owl.

"Hey guys, are you okay down there?" Hira asked.

"We heard rumours that it's Bonfire Night tonight and we really don't like the fireworks," Ru squeaked in a wobbly voice. "It's even louder in this echoey garage, but we've got nowhere else to go and we're afraid."

"Well, we can't have that, can we?" Hira said as she picked up some sticks with her paws. "We're building a den in the house and you are welcome to join us."

"Bring your friends and families," Albert added. "No animal should be afraid on Bonfire Night."

Later that evening, there was a tapping on the dog flap and Ru and Ali pushed their way inside.

Soon the whole living room was filled with friends from the great outdoors. Everyone came. Mr Phillips the fox and his six cubs. The rats from the next village, Bella the badger from over the hedge and at least three generations of local hedgehogs. Miranda and Mo Magpie turned up with some honeycomb they had just swiped from an open kitchen window.

Then the front door went – the lady butler was home. But as soon as she walked into the living room, she screamed, dropped her keys and ran straight out again, flapping her arms as she went.

"Our butler must hate fireworks more than I do," said Albert.

Then all the animals squeezed into the den and had a lovely time, laughing and eating honeycomb and definitely not hearing any noisy fireworks.

Sparkles and bangs tell us that it's November 5th and Bonfire Night! It marks the day in 1605 when a plot to cause an explosion in the Houses of Parliament was discovered and stopped.

NOISY HONEYCOMB BITS

These are fizzy, poppy, crunchy fun. You can dip the honeycomb in chocolate or you can eat it without a coating – just make sure it is cool before you tuck in!

Makes about 40 pieces, depending on shape and size

Ingredients

sunflower oil, for the baking trays

200g caster sugar

4 tbsp golden syrup

3 tsp bicarbonate of soda

200g milk chocolate

popping candy, to decorate

Method

- Line two large baking trays with baking paper and oil them very lightly.

- Put the sugar and the golden syrup into a large, deep, non-stick saucepan. Boiling sugar is dangerous, so be extra careful and pay special attention.

- Cook the mixture over a medium heat for 6 minutes, carefully swirling the pan to dissolve the sugar (don't stir it). You will know it is ready when the sugar has melted and it is a brown amber colour. Take off the heat and set aside.

- Add the bicarbonate of soda to the pan and mix it in really quickly. The mixture will start bubbling and fizzing to the top of the pan.

- Being very careful, pour the mixture into the prepared trays and watch it as it moves outwards and spreads. Don't touch the mixture as it is still very hot. Leave the honeycomb to cool completely.

- When it is cold and hard, break the honeycomb into pieces. You will get big pieces and small pieces – that's okay.

- Put the milk chocolate in a microwavable bowl and microwave for 1 minute. Stir, then microwave in 10-second bursts, stirring each time, until the chocolate is liquid.

- Dip half of each piece of honeycomb into the melted chocolate and sprinkle with the popping candy.

- Lay the pieces on some fresh baking paper and wait for the chocolate to set before eating.

Nadiya's tip:
If you can't find popping candy, you can use coloured sprinkles instead. Why not wrap some honeycomb in cellophane, tie it with ribbon and give it as a gift to friends?

SALTED-CARAMEL PANCAKES

These are perfect for warming you up after outdoor Bonfire Night celebrations. They are thick American pancakes with a yummy filling that will ooze out when cut.

Makes 14-16

Ingredients

3 medium eggs

100g caster sugar

150ml whole milk

300g self-raising flour

50g unsalted butter, melted
  oil spray

small pot (220g) of ready-made salted caramel spread (you only need 14-16 heaped tsp for this recipe)

1 tbsp icing sugar, for dusting

Method

* Put the eggs and sugar into a large bowl and whisk with a handheld whisk until combined. Whisk in the milk.

* Now add the flour and keep whisking until you have a thick batter. Pour in the melted butter and mix.

* Put a non-stick frying pan over a medium to low heat and oil it very lightly with the oil spray.

* Add 2 tablespoons of the batter to the frying pan. Cook the pancake for 3–4 minutes.

* Add 1 heaped teaspoon of the salted caramel on top.

* Now add 1 teaspoon more of the batter on top, to just cover the caramel, then carefully flip the pancake over with a spatula.

* Cook for another 2–3 minutes, until golden on both sides and the batter is cooked through.

* Keep each pancake on a foil-covered plate to keep them warm while you cook the rest.

* Sift a little icing sugar over all of them before eating.

> Nadiya's tip:
> If you want to save time,
> make the batter the night
> before, then cover and leave
> it in the fridge.

FIREWORKS IN A JAR

You will need:

200ml water

400ml jar with a lid, cleaned

food colouring of your choice

200ml vegetable oil

1 tsp glitter of your choice (I like to
mix 2 colours, so ½ tsp of each)

To make:

Pour the water into the jar.
Add a few drops of food
colouring so the water is just
slightly coloured.

Mix the oil and glitter in a
small jug.

Add the glitter mixture to the
jar, screw on the lid and leave
to settle.

When you want a burst of
fireworks, give the jar a shake,
then watch the colourful
fireworks happen.

Hanukkah
THE LOST KITTEN

Noah and Nibbles

were best friends. Nibbles slept on Noah's bed at night, and woke him up every morning with a gentle snuffle and a purr. Nibbles even tried to hide in Noah's backpack so she could go to school with him, but Mum always scooped her out before Noah left the house.

One morning, Noah woke up without Nibbles purring in his ear. He was worried. It was the first day of Hanukkah, and he wanted to celebrate it with Nibbles.

"Don't worry, Noah," Dad said, "Nibbles is probably busy with her own Hanukkah celebrations with the neighbourhood cats. She'll be back soon."

But Nibbles hadn't come back by the time Noah returned from school. Noah was really worried now. He sat at the window, looking out at the street, wishing and hoping he would see Nibbles sauntering up the street towards the house.

Noah was so worried that he couldn't eat all the delicious fried Hanukkah treats that

he'd been looking forward to for weeks.
His granny placed a plate of potato latkes
in front of him, fresh from the pan. Noah
had one half-hearted mouthful. Granny
eventually took the plate away.

Next, she tried with a doughnut. It was warm and sweet and rolled in cinnamon. Noah tried a bite, to make Granny happy, but he just wasn't hungry. Granny ate the doughnut herself.

Night fell, and Noah was still sat at the window.

"How will Nibbles be able to find her way home in the dark?" he cried to his dad.

"I tell you what," said Dad. "Why don't we light a tealight together, and place it in the window to help guide her home?"

Dad scrabbled in a drawer and found a tealight. There was only one left.

"Oh dear," said Dad, shaking his head. "I knew there was something I was supposed to buy this week."

"Dad! What if the tealight goes out?" Noah said.

"Well, we can use this tonight and we can go and buy some more tomorrow," Dad said, reassuringly, and they placed the candle in a safe spot on the windowsill.

The next morning, Noah rushed downstairs. No Nibbles. Noah headed for his place at the the window, but when he got there, he gasped. The little tealight was still burning brightly. *Tealights don't normally last that long, do they ...?* Noah wondered, as he picked up his backpack and headed to school.

That night, Nibbles still hadn't returned. But the tealight continued to burn! Granny had been keeping an eye on it all day, and Dad checked it was safe before they all went to bed.

Noah went to sleep with a heavy heart.

Six more days without Nibbles passed, and Noah got sadder and sadder. But the tealight continued to burn, which made him feel just a tiny bit better. Then, just before bedtime on the eighth day after Nibbles went missing, Noah heard a faint "meow" outside his bedroom window. He raced downstairs. His best friend was back!

Noah flung open the door and scooped Nibbles into a cuddle. It was the best cuddle of his life. Nibbles licked Noah's face and purred in his ear.

The best friends settled down in front of a plate of Granny's fried Hanukkah treats, and as Nibbles meowed the stories of her adventures to Noah, the little boy glanced over at the window.

The tealight that had burned for eight whole days had finally gone out.

POTATO LATKES

You can buy latkes frozen, but it is so much more fun to make your own. This is such a simple recipe and so delicious that it makes me love potatoes even more than I already do!

Makes 10

Ingredients

2 potatoes (300g), scrubbed and grated with skin still on

½ tsp salt

pepper

1 medium egg, lightly beaten

4 tbsp plain flour, or matzo meal

1 tsp baking powder

sunflower oil, for frying

Nadiya's tip:
If you prefer sweet potatoes, you can use them in place of white potatoes. The method is exactly the same.

Method

* Take a handful of grated potato, wrap it in a clean tea towel and squeeze out as much liquid as you can over the sink. Shake the dry potato out into a bowl. Repeat until all the potato is squeezed out.

* Add the salt and pepper to the bowl and mix.

* Add the egg and mix again, then add the flour and baking powder and stir until the potato mixture forms a thick clump.

* Put 2 tablespoons of oil into a large non-stick frying pan and place over a medium heat until hot.

* Take 1 heaped tablespoon of the potato mixture and gently place it in the pan. Using the back of a spoon, flatten the latke. Try to get 4–5 latkes in the pan, but don't squash them in.

* Leave to fry over a medium to low heat for 5 minutes on each side until golden brown and crisp. This will make them much easier to turn over with a spatula. Drain each latke on some kitchen paper.

* Continue with the remaining mixture to make 10 latkes in total, adding a little extra oil as necessary to the pan. You will need to do this in 2–3 batches.

CINNAMON DOUGHNUTS

This recipe can be a real team effort in the kitchen, especially if baking with siblings. A grown-up should handle the frying, but one child can cut out the pastry shapes, another can mix the spices and sugar, then everyone can have a go at rolling the doughnuts in the mixture. Yum!

Makes 12

Ingredients

320g ready-rolled puff pastry

sunflower oil, for deep-frying

100g caster sugar

1 tsp ground cinnamon

You will also need

8cm round pastry cutter

Method

✳ Find a baking tray that fits in your freezer. This needs to be ready for when you cut out the pastry.

✳ Roll the pastry out a little more on a work surface and, using an 8cm cutter, stamp out 12 circles. Leftover pastry can be re-rolled and made into smaller doughnuts.

✳ Pop the circles onto the baking tray and freeze for just 15 minutes. This will help the doughnuts to keep their shape when frying.

✳ Now line a tray with some kitchen paper to mop up any excess oil after frying.

✳ Place a large non-stick frying pan or deep sauté pan over a high heat. Add the oil to a depth of about 1cm.

✳ To test if the oil is hot enough, take a small chunk of bread and drop it into the pan. If it sizzles to the top, the oil is ready.

✳ Carefully place the pastry circles in the hot oil, a few at a time, keeping the rest of the circles in the freezer to keep them cool.

✳ Fry on each side for 1–1½ minutes, then place onto the prepared kitchen paper. They should be light golden brown, crisp and cooked through.

✳ Mix the sugar and cinnamon on a plate and give it a good mix.

✳ Take a doughnut and roll it around in the mixture until every last bit is covered in cinnamon sugar. Repeat with the rest of the doughnuts.

> **Nadiya's tip:**
> There are so many ways you can flavour sugar. You could replace the cinnamon with the grated zest of an orange, or use 1 teaspoon of freshly grated nutmeg instead.

PAPER FLAMES

You will need:

sheets of red, yellow and orange card

scissors

glue

To make:

Choose which colour you want your biggest flame to be. Cut a sheet of card of this colour in half lengthways, then fold one of the halves concertina style.

Draw a flame shape on the top layer of the concertina, making sure both sides of the shape are touching both folded edges of the card.

Cut around the shape, being careful not to cut along the edges that touch the folds.

Carefully unfold your paper chain.

Cut out smaller flame shapes from the other colours and glue them onto the big flames.

You can use your flames to decorate a Hanukkah table, or anywhere else that needs something colourful to brighten it up!

Thank you

Thanks to my chief taste-testers and all-round critics, Musa, Dawud and Maryam. Your truth-telling never ceases to amaze me. Keep being honest, no matter how much I don't want to hear it! But most of all, thank you for listening to every single story. Reading to you guys is a joy, and one that I may not have forever, so thank you for your time and your ears.

Thank you so much, Emma Goldhawk, for sticking with me to the very end. Our email exchanges and parcel deliveries have led us to three incredible books we can be so proud of! Without your help and constant guidance, my goodness, this would have been so much harder. Simply, you are a joy!

Thank you to Fritha Lindqvist, for sticking it out with me. I am married to the list writer of all list writers and you surpass him! You are so precise and measured that nothing ever feels like a chore.

Thank you Claire Rossiter. I give you a story and you always surpass the images in my head with your illustrations. The smiles, the eyes, the characters – they all breath life into my words.

Thank you, Alison, for your beautiful design. Your ideas and direction have brought such energy into every single page of this book.

Thank you to everyone at Hodder Children's Books and Hachette Children's Group: Bhavini, Sarah, Becky, Anne, Katy, Lucy, Nic, Jane and Hilary. You guys worked so hard to make this book happen. I appreciate it so much.

And thank you to all the people who have supported my Bake Me a Story books. Without my little cooks and readers, these books would be nothing. They are what they are because the kid in me would have loved a book like this, and I am delighted that so many of you have enjoyed them.

Never forget to use your hands and your imaginations. Bake, make and be happy. And of course, always find an excuse to celebrate.

Nadiya